Terry Tarbox worked for many years in the retail furniture trade, but has also been a postman, a milkman, an ice-cream seller and manager of a Pet cemetery (a job he soon decided was not for him).

Now retired, his hobbies are gardening, reading and writing.

He blames *Spike Milligan, The Goon Show* and *Monty Python's Flying Circus* for the level of humour in his tall tales and rhymes.

Born and brought up in North London, he now lives in Lowestoft, Suffolk.

Also by Terry Tarbox

The Willigrews
(Seriously Silly Stories for Children)

Available from

www.willigrews.co.uk

and

Amazon

MY MATE JOE
AND
OTHER RHYMES

Terry Tarbox

First published in England in 2013 by Createspace for Amazon

Copyright © Terry Tarbox 2013

Illustrations by WW Design
ww.design@btinternet.com
01825 768518

ISBN 978-1490979649

Dedication

This book is dedicated to

Wendy Wheatley

whose wonderful illustrations bring my characters to life

CONTENTS

LILY BROWN

Lily Brown went into town to buy a bag of sweets,
Her mum had sent her shopping all looking nice and neat,
But she fell into a puddle and spoiled her pretty dress,
She looked down at her clothes and said,
"Oh! What a soggy mess."

TOBY DOBIE'S WOOD

The rain was really pouring down in Toby Dobie's Wood,
The weather for some days now had not been very good.
The creatures that lived there, sheltered 'neath the boughs,
Three squirrels, five hedgehogs and half a dozen cows.

They wondered when the rain would stop in Toby Dobie's Wood.
They couldn't even go in search to find themselves some food,
The hedgehogs had eaten all the slugs the squirrels all the nuts,
The cows were mooing ceaselessly 'cos the grass had all been cut.

They could not wait until it grew for they would surely starve,
And one of them, called Daisybelle, was just about to calve.
They couldn't go for help because the rain was falling hard,
They wished they hadn't left the safety of the farmer's yard.

A cow said, "One of us must go for help!" A hedgehog said, "Not me!"
None of the squirrels fancied it and legged it up the tree,
Daisybelle was now in trouble; the calf was coming at the double,
Fearing for their bovine friend, the others gathered in a huddle.

The expectant mum was very stressed and began to wander round.
The others thought she needed peace so didn't make a sound.
They held their breaths and waited; it didn't look like fun,
Then in a flash the calf was born; it came out with the sun.

They gathered in the sunshine, so happy for their friend.
It's funny how things turn out well, on that we can depend.
They all went home back to the farm, so glad that fate was kind,
Happy now because the little calf was following on behind.

Now the moral of this story is, well there never was one really,
The hedgehogs and the squirrels were wild animals quite clearly,
This story happened in my head, though I was glad to tell it,
They had no midwifery skills; they couldn't even spell it!

A HAIRY DOG CALLED KNOBBLYKNEES

A hairy dog called Knobblyknees
Was running very fast.
He ran even faster when he saw a cat go past,
He was gaining on the pussy cat and getting very close,
But he ran into a lamp post,
And squashed his little nose.

LITTLE DORA DINGBAT

Little Dora Dingbat sat upon a rock.
While she was sitting, she got a nasty shock.
A big hairy spider landed on her head,
So she screamed a bit and ran a lot,
Then went back home to bed.

THE SNAPPERDACK

One sunny day in a far away land
A family of pixies was waiting for the band.
A grand parade was due to pass and they were very pleased,
But a nasty snapperdack came down and bit off all their knees.

"Come back at once," they cried, "You horrid little thing!"
At first they couldn't chase it, 'cos snapperdacks have wings,
The Snapperdack then flew away, the knees held in its mouth.
"We'll follow it," one pixie said, "I think it's heading south."

The chase was very tiring; it seemed to have no end.
The Pixies walked stiff-legged as their knees they couldn't bend,
But the Snapperdack had landed, which wasn't very smart,
The Pixies found him sitting on a pile of body parts.

The Pixies ran up to the bones and said, "Look, they're our knees!"
One said to the Snapperdack, "May we have them please?"
The Snapperdack said, "No you can't I'm making a collection;
I just need a donkey's hip bone, then I'll have a full selection."

One pixie said, "Please return them now as we did ask you politely.
If you don't give us back our knees we shall not take it lightly!"
The Snapperdack then gave a hoot and snappered with his beak,
The Pixies soon decided that there wasn't time to speak.

The Monster made a grab for them and bit a pixie's toe,
The Pixies stood together and shouted out, "OH NO!"
They cast a shower of pixie dust on the Snapperdack that day,
And it turned into a hamster and quickly ran away.

LITTLE SIMON SLEEPYNOSE

Little Simon Sleepynose was sitting on a swing.
While he was swinging, he saw a funny thing,
A hedgehog on a skateboard went scooting by.
It slowed a bit and waved a bit,
And winked its little eye.

8

LITTLE SIDNEY HAIRYEARS

Little Sidney Hairyears was looking for his mate.
He said that he would meet him and thought he would be late.
It was very cold outside; his feet were going numb.
He ran across some slippery mud,
And fell down on his bum.

LONG, LONG AGO

Long, long ago in a land far away,
All the little children had forgotten how to play.
Their toys were left, neglected, lying on the ground;
No laughs, no happy shouts, they didn't make a sound.

Peter said to Mary, "I wonder what is wrong?"
Mary said, "I don't know; I can't even sing a song."
"I know," said Peter, "let us scream and shout!"
But when they tried Mary cried, as no sound would come out.

All the Children walked about not knowing what to do,
"I can't remember what we did," said Mary. "How about you?"
"I can't recall a single game," sad Peter then replied.
Then all the little Children sat on the ground and cried.

Then up came farmer Hairynose, who asked them what was wrong,
"Why aren't you playing with your toys; why don't you sing a song?"
"We can't remember how to sing," He heard the Children say.
"We'd love to dance about, but we've forgotten how to play."

Just then a horrid Witch appeared from just behind a tree,
The children gasped in fear and fright, the Witch said, "Look at me,
I have cast a spell on you, and you will play no more,
Your noise brought on my migraine and made my poor head sore."

The Farmer ran towards the Witch. He was looking very mad,
"I will not let you do this you ugly looking hag!"
He pushed her down; her hat fell off; he grabbed her by the throat.
But with one small wave of the Witch's hand he turned into a goat.

Just then, a fairy fluttered down she said. "My name is Toots."
They couldn't help but notice she was wearing hobnail boots.
The boots were very heavy, and she landed with a thud.
She turned to face the Witch and said, "This isn't very good."

With swirling wings and rainbow dust, which made the Children clap,
She cast a spell upon the Witch with one almighty zap.
The Witch ran around in circles and jumping up and down,
She fell into the lake and screamed, "Help, I'm gonna drown!"

But, as she hit the water, she turned into a trout,
She swam away quite gracefully (still angry there's no doubt).
The Fairy then turned to the children to lift the Witch's spell,
A sparkling shower of pink and green upon the Children fell.

As for farmer Hairynose, he turned back into a man.
His nose no longer hairy he had to change his name.
Now if you were passing through this place, you'd have to smile and say,
How happy all these Children are to sing and dance at play.

A BOY CALLED JACK

A boy called Jack, who had a cough,
Coughed so hard his head fell off!
His head went down a slippery hill
And rolled into a flour mill.
The Miller said, "I've found a head,
I think I'll turn it into bread."
The head said, "NO, my name is Jack;
I need to get my body back."
The Miller laughed and said, "OK,
I'll take you back, I know the way."

"Be careful please," the head complained.
"Don't run you're shaking up my brain!"
Upon the hill, the body found,
Just lying helpless on the ground,
The Miller put Jack's head back on.
Jack thanked the Miller then went home,
Now all was well, Jack was delighted,
Head and body reunited.

THE SQUIRREL HUNT

I went on a squirrel hunt
With my very best friend Rose.
She grabbed a squirrel by the tail
And it bit her on the nose.

FIFTY P

Fifty p, fifty p,
Is all I have to spend on me.
I could spend it on some treats;
I would love a bag of sweets.

But Mum would say, "Don't waste your money.
Spend it on some bread and honey,
Honey's very good for you,
It might protect you from the Flu."

What to do, what to do?
You'd have to wonder wouldn't you?
I know I'll toss the coin to see,
Which way up it lands for me.

Heads for bread, tails for sweets
Each would my desires meet.
Oops! I've dropped it down a drain,
I'll never see that coin again!

Feeling sad, feeling sorry,
I miss my money very sorely,
Oh no, now I'm sneezing too!
I think I might have caught the Flu.

Now that I have lost my money,
I wish I'd bought the bread and honey.
I guess I'll have to wander home,
And tell my Mum what I have done.

When I got home Mum dosed me up.
She gave me mixture in a cup.
She said, "Now drink it and don't pout,"
It tasted just like sour kraut.

Mum didn't scold me in the end,
She'll wait until I'm on the mend,
That's what she did once in the past,
I'd better make this illness last.

THE SAUSAGE AND THE SPROUT

One day near our local tip,
A sausage met a sprout.
They fell in love quite instantly,
Of that there was no doubt.

Sausage said to Sprout his love,
"Oh let us run away."
Sprout replied, "Yes please my dear,
Forever and a day."

They bounced along so happily,
The Sausage and the Sprout.
They crossed a field and found a wood,
Where they hoped they could hide out.

"Nobody will find us here,"
I heard the sausage say.
"We'll build a home and never roam,
Together we will stay."

As sausages and sprouts don't eat,
No need to search for food,
And nobody would eat them here,
They'd be happy here for good.

But not long after, Sprout fell ill,
This made poor sausage worry,
"I'll have to fetch a doctor, Dear,"
Said he and ran off in a hurry.

He found a vegetable doctor,
In the yellow pages.
He made the call quite urgently,
But had to wait for ages.

16

At last the Doctor answered,
Said he'd come out straight away,
"It's on the NHS now,
So you shouldn't have to pay."

The Doc examined Sprout and said,
"You're suffering from a fungus.
If I don't help you'll swell and swell,
In fact you'll be humungous."

Looking on in anguish Sausage said,
"What can you do?
I just can't live without my Sprout.
I'd be lonely and so blue."

The Doctor pulled an aerosol,
From within his leather bag,
Then sprayed it gently over Sprout
Telling Sausage not to nag.

They had to wait a little while
To see if the spray had helped.
Then Sprout started moving,
Jumped up and down and yelped.

Sprout said, "I'm feeling better now."
And hopping up and down,
The Sausage did a little jig.
They all danced round and round.

They thanked the Doctor gratefully,
His work completed, he went home
With the Sausage and the Sprout so happy,
Never ever more to roam.

SKINNY JIM

A boy named Jim was frightfully thin,
So they gave him extra dinner.
His appetite was very poor,
So he just kept getting thinner.

His Mum had tried most everything,
Like pork and eggs and custard.
She even made ham sandwiches,
With a little touch of mustard.

She had become quite desperate
To get something past his lips,
So she decided one cold evening,
To try some fish and chips

She wrapped up warm and left the house,
And went to the local Chippy.
She had to walk quite carefully,
'Cos the pavements were quite slippy.

She fell down once, but got back up.
She walked a bit and fell down twice,
Yet holding on to the fish and chips,
She started skating on the ice.

Once she'd got going she got home fast,
Jim welcomed her as she got in.
"I've bought you fish and chips my dear,
This will stop you being thin."

Jim opened the wrapping and looked inside.
He sniffed the air and liked what he smelt.
"This looks quite tasty," he said to his Mum,
He ate a few chips and declared that he felt...

Like eating again. So he got stuck in
Like a thing possessed he was munching away.
He finished it all and looked at his Mum,
"I'd love some more Mum; what do you say?"

His Mum was excited; he was eating at last.
She went back to the Chippy and ordered more fast.
She had ten helpings under her arm,
So Jim got stuck in to this hefty repast.

Jim scoffed the food, without a pause,
When he would stop there was no telling,
His Mum started fretting; he was eating too quickly,
She was very concerned as his stomach was swelling.

Out of control now, this food was so tasty,
He piled the grub on. His plate was quite loaded.
Poor Jim couldn't stop. If his Mum hadn't made him,
He might have kept eating and would have exploded.

MY MATE JOE

I had a pet snail,
His name was Joe.
I would take him for walks,
Though he was rather slow.

We'd walk for miles,
(Well, inches really).
He was my best mate,
And I loved him dearly.

He didn't talk much,
So neither did I.
We'd converse with each other,
By winking an eye.

Mine in a socket,
His on a tentacle
Apart from those things,
We were almost identical.

Until one day,
When I'd left him alone.
Without my protection,
He was all on his own.

He saw some blue food,
He was going to scoff it.
I ran very fast,
To try put him off it.

I shouted to Joe,
"Please don't eat that Mate."
I hoped that my warning,
Wasn't too late.

He stopped in his tracks
And looked up at me.
"It's poisoned," I said.
He had to agree.

"The people who hate you,
Have put pellets down.
So never eat blue food,"
I said with a frown.

Joe knew what I meant,
But he didn't talk.
He just winked his eye,
And we went for a walk.

"The people," I said,
"Who are all out to get you,
Don't know what you're like,
'Cos they've never met you."

ABEL JONES

There was a man called Abel Jones
Who spent his whole life on his own.
Old Abel was a hairy hermit,
Seriously, he had a permit!
He never shaved, he never washed,
He spent his time just smelling.
But he would say he didn't smell,
'Cos there was no one around to smell him.

THE DOG ON THE LOG

I once knew a Dog that ate a Frog
And sat there croaking on a log.
Some other frogs that saw the Dog
Said, "Why is it croaking like a frog?"
The Frog hopped about in the poor Dog's tum
And made the pooch feel very glum.
"I wish I'd never eaten it," said the Dog,
"It's made me feel quite sick."
Then the Dog gave one almighty vomit
And the Frog flew out with goo upon it.
The only other thing that happened that day,
The Frog jumped in the pond and swam away.

MARY

A girl called Mary, who worked in a dairy
Saw a beautiful milk white Fairy,
The Fairy said, "Hello Mary I'm not scary,
I'm always kind, I never vary.
Are you the Mary that was quite contrary?"
"No, I'm the Mary who works in the dairy,"
As she was a kindly Fairy
And the day was light and airy,
She gave our Mary her canary.
Then Mary went back to the dairy.

THE CAT AND THE SPARROW

A little black cat was sitting on a wall,
When a chirpy little sparrow paid him a call.
"I suppose I should eat you now," I heard the Cat say,
"But I'm not all that keen on doing things that way.
I'm not like that."

"The truth is I'm too lazy and I've never liked to fight.
I just like sleeping and howling through the night.
That upsets all the neighbours, it really is great fun.
They sometimes throw things at us. Once someone threw a bun.
I liked that."

"We shared the bun out equally, Spike and Sam and I.
We had a sleep and then continued squealing at the sky.
Oh I did chase a bird once, but when it stopped I froze.
The cheeky thing flew straight at me and pecked me on the nose.
I didn't like that."

Out of interest the Cat asked "What type of buns d'you like?
The Bird replied quite rudely, "I'd best be on me bike."
The tiny Sparrow gave a chirp and flew up to the sky,
The little Cat was a little miffed 'cos it didn't say." Goodbye."
How do you like that?

ZACH AND THE BEANSTALK

A boy called Zach, who grew too big,
Had almost lost the will to live.
Everyone was getting smaller
While poor old Zach kept getting taller.

He went to see his family Doctor,
But she thought he was off his rocker,
Said, "Come back when you've got the flu.
Then I will know just what to do."

Zach grew taller every day.
He couldn't carry on this way!
He couldn't even walk through doors;
He wished that there were lower floors.

Others started taunting him,
Him so tall and very thin.
Their comments drove him to despair,
Like, "What's the weather like up there?"

"I've had enough of this," thought Zach,
"How can I get my shortness back?
I know, I'll go and see this bloke,
I doubt he'll treat it as a joke."

So he went along to Wiseman Fred,
Who lived in his next door neighbour's shed.
He couldn't quite get through the door,
So he had to get down on all fours.

Zach poked his head inside the door
And saw old Fred sitting on the floor.
"Can you help me, Mate, I'm growing fast?"
Fred said, "I thought that it was overcast.

Good grief! You're blocking out the sun.
Your problem can't be that much fun.
You'll have to tell me what you've eaten,
If you can't remember then we're beaten."

"On Monday I had sausage and mash,.
On Tuesday I had corned beef hash.
On Wednesday I had pork and greens
And on Thursday I had lamb and beans."

Fred asked, "Now, were they runner beans?
Cos' sometimes they aren't what they seem.
Are you sure that they were properly cooked?
Open your mouth and I'll take a look."

Zach opened wide, and Fred espied
A bean shoot about a half inch wide.
"It's pushing up your head," said Fred,
"Another inch and you'll be dead.

Hold tight while I just cut it off,
But do beware it may make you cough!"
With sharp scissors, Fred gave a clip,
Then three more cuts went snip, snip, snip!

Because the beans weren't properly done.
One took root inside Zach's tum.
It grew and grew beyond its scope,
Zach opened like a telescope.

Fred pulled the plant out from Zach's throat,
Trying not to make him choke.
Now Zach was as happy as can be,
And rushed home to tell his family.

BILLY SQUEERS WHO LOST HIS EARS

A little boy named Billy Squeers,
Woke up to find he'd lost his ears.
"That's very strange," young Billy said,
"I had them when I went to bed."

His Mum said, "Bill you silly thing,
Why are you always losing things?
Tell me when did you last see 'em?
Hang on a sec though; this might be 'em."

She put her hand beneath the bed,
The mouse she found was very dead.
She took it to the window ledge
And hurled it swiftly off the edge.

Then someone shouted from below,
"Something just hit me on the nose,
This really is the strangest thing,
There's a bat down here without its wings."

"You stupid twit," Bill's Mum replied,
"It's just a mouse grew old and died."
"Poor little thing just lying there,
I'll bury it and say a prayer."

"Suit yourself," Bill's mother said,
And continued looking neath the bed,
"Come on and help me Billy dear,"
He ignored her cos, he had no ears.

She looked in every nook and cranny.
Then in came little Billy's Granny.
"Would these be what you're looking for?
I found them on the bathroom floor."

"Come over here your ears are back,
I'll stick 'em on with some Blu Tack.
I'm sure that this will do for you,
Till I can buy some Super Glue.

Dear Reader

If you have enjoyed reading these rhymes,
please leave a review on Amazon

You can follow me on
www.willigrews.co.uk
facebook
or
twitter

I welcome your comments and would love to hear from you

13699736R00025

Printed in Poland
by Amazon Fulfillment
Poland Sp. z o.o., Wrocław